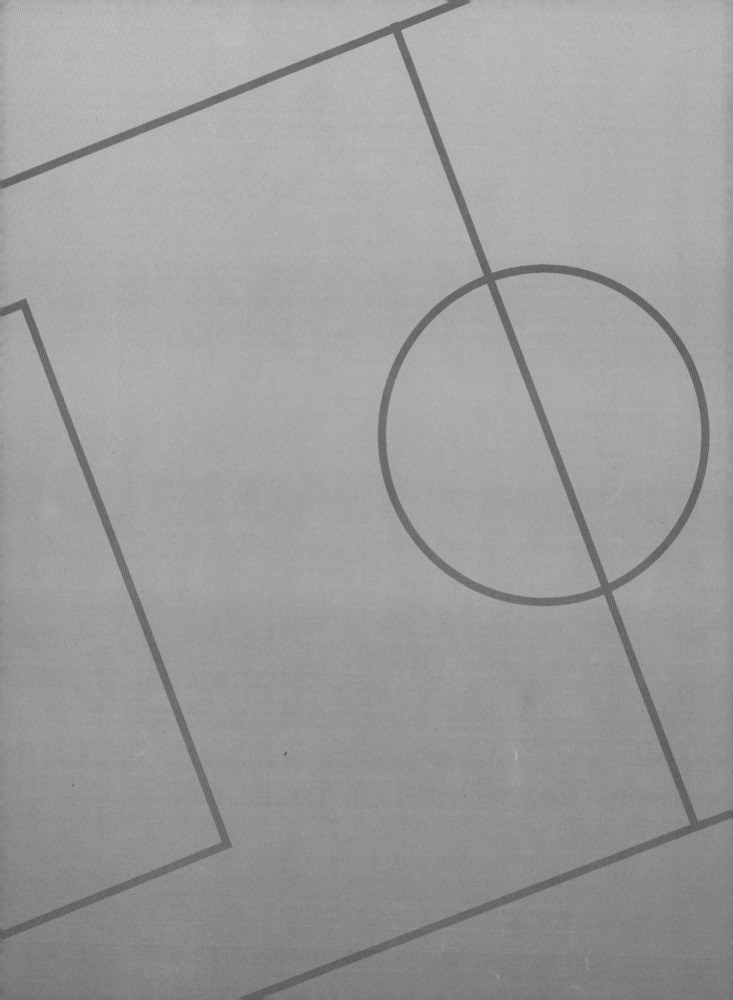

KNOW YOUR SPORT

Soccer

Clive Gifford

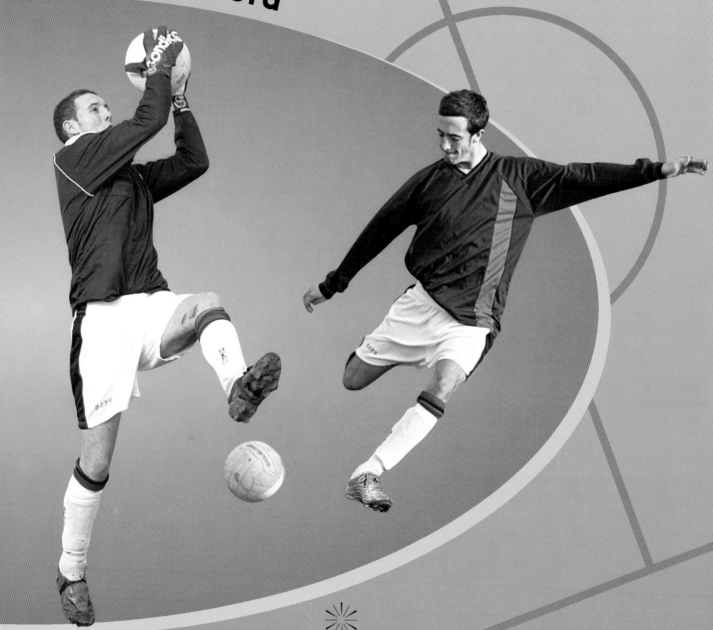

SEA-TO-SEA

Mankato Collingwood London

This edition first published in 2009 by
Sea-to-Sea Publications
Distributed by Black Rabbit Books
P.O. Box 3263
Mankato, Minnesota 56002

Library of Congress Cataloging-in-Publication Data:

Gifford, Clive.
  Soccer / Clive Gifford.
    p. cm. -- (Know your sport)
  Summary: "Describes the equipment, training, moves, and
competitions of soccer. Includes step-by-step descriptions of moves"--
Provided by publisher.
  Includes index.
  ISBN 978-1-59771-152-4
  1. Soccer--Juvenile literature. I. Title.
  GV943.25.G549 2009
  796.334--dc22
                                        2008007320

9 8 7 6 5 4 3 2

Published by arrangement with the Watts
Publishing Group Ltd, London.

Series editor: Jennifer Schofield
Art director: Jonathan Hair

**Series designed and created for Franklin Watts
by Painted Fish Ltd.**
Designer: Rita Storey
Editor: Nicola Edwards
Photography: Tudor Photography, Banbury

Note: At the time of going to press, the statistics
and players' profiles in this book were up to date.
However, due to some soccer players' active
participation in the sport,
it is possible that some of these may now be
out of date.

Picture credits

Action plus/Glyn Kirk p.6; Action plus/
Howard C. Smith/Icon p.8; Action plus/Neil
Tingle p.8 (right); Icon/Action plus p.10; Action
plus/Neil Tingle p.12; Action plus/Neil Tingle
p.13; Action plus/Glyn Kirk p.18; Action
plus/Glyn Kirk p.21; Action plus/Neil Tingle p.
23; Action plus/Neil Tingle p.25; Action
plus/Richard Frances p26.

Cover images: Tudor Photography, Banbury.

All photos posed by models.
Thanks to Matthew Carberry, Mark Fenemore,
Henry Glendinning, Yannick Nkwanyvo, Charlie
Storey, and Carl Taylor.

The Publisher would like to thank Banbury
school for the use of its soccer field.

Taking part in a sport
is a fun way to get in shape, but
like any form of physical
exercise it has an element of
risk, particularly if you are unfit,
overweight, or suffer from any
medical conditions. It is advisable
to consult a healthcare
professional before beginning
any program
of exercise.

Contents

Introduction

Soccer is the world's most popular sport. Hundreds of millions of people across the globe either watch or play this all-action game. No single individual invented the sport. Games played with a ball and feet have existed all over the world for hundreds of years, but soccer, as we know it, began in the nineteenth century.

The Aim of the Game

A soccer game lasts 90 minutes, divided into two 45-minute halves. There are 11 players on each team, some of whom can be replaced during a match by substitutes.

Players can use any parts of their bodies to move the ball around the field—except their arms and their hands. (The exception is the goalkeeper—see pages 26–27.) The aim of the game is to score goals. A goal is awarded by the referee—the official who runs the game—when the ball completely crosses the goal-line between the two goalposts. The team with more goals at the end of the game wins the match.

The Field

A full-sized soccer field is between 295 and 394 feet (90-120 meters) long and 147–295 feet (45-90 meters) wide. Its edges are bounded by long sidelines and, at each end of the field, goal linee.A halfway line divides the field in two. In the middle of this line is a center spot, where the ball is placed before a game begins.

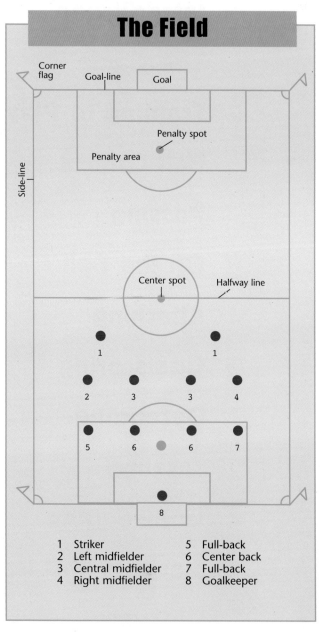

The Field

Corner flag
Goal-line
Goal
Penalty spot
Penalty area
Side-line
Center spot
Halfway line

1	Striker	5	Full-back
2	Left midfielder	6	Center back
3	Central midfielder	7	Full-back
4	Right midfielder	8	Goalkeeper

There are 11 players on each team, including the goalkeeper, strikers, midfielders, and backs (also known as defenders). Strikers are the players that usually score goals while the backs mainly defend, making sure opponents do not score goals. Players in the midfield can play either defense or attack, depending on the rest of the team.

Restarting the Game

When the whole of the ball crosses the sideline or goal line and leaves the field, the game stops. Play can be restarted in a number of ways depending on where the ball went out and which side touched it last. For example, if the ball crosses the goal line and the attacking team touched it last, a goal kick is awarded to the defending team.

Soccer for All

The beauty of soccer is that it is a simple sport that needs little equipment. Informal games can be held in parks or even in a street with fewer than 11 players on each side. One of the most popular smaller versions is five-a-side, often played indoors in a gym. Five- and seven-a-side games are great ways to build up skills and fitness to play the full game.

Taking a Throw-in

Fanatical Fans

Soccer is so popular that an estimated 1.1 billion people watched the 2002 World Cup. Some people even painted their houses in their team colors to show their support.

Taking a Corner

▲

If the ball completely crosses a sideline, a throw-in is awarded to the team who did not touch the ball last. To perform a throw-in, the player must keep his feet on the ground and behind the side line. Both hands must be kept on the ball as he brings it back over his head and then forward to release it into play.

▶ If the ball crosses the goal line, then a corner is awarded if the defending team touched it last. The ball is placed in the corner quadrant and the player will look to pass short to a teammate or cross it toward the goal to create an attack.

The Game

Soccer games are run according to the Laws of the Game. The referee is the person who controls the game with the help of two assistants who run along the sidelines.

The Referee's Duties

The referee makes sure a game is played within the Laws of the Game. It is up to the referee to decide if a goal has been scored or whether to award a free kick or penalty. The referee's decision is always final. The referee is also responsible for timekeeping.

Foul!

Fouls include tripping, kicking, pushing, and pulling on a shirt to hold back an opponent. The referee punishes a foul by awarding a free kick to the other team. If the foul takes place inside the penalty area, the punishment is usually a penalty kick.

Red and Yellow Cards

Apart from a whistle, the referee has two other important pieces of equipment: a yellow and a red card. If a bad foul is committed, the referee can "book" or "caution" the player responsible by raising the yellow card. An even more serious foul can result in a red card, which means a player is "sent off." He has to leave the field and his side plays with one player fewer for the rest of the game. According to the Laws of the Game, a player who receives two yellow cards during the course of a match is automatically sent off.

Free kicks

There are two types of free kick. A direct free kick can be struck straight at goal.
An indirect free kick has to be touched by another player first. Free kicks close to the other team's goal are a really good chance to score a goal.

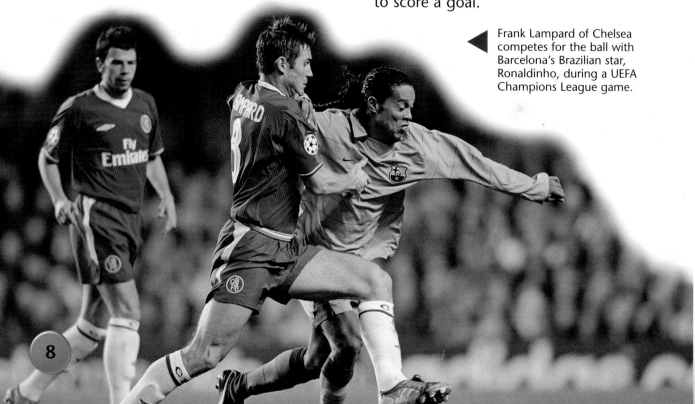

Frank Lampard of Chelsea competes for the ball with Barcelona's Brazilian star, Ronaldinho, during a UEFA Champions League game.

On the Spot

A penalty kick is taken from the penalty spot, a little under 40 ft (12 m) from the goal-line. Only the penalty-taker and the goalkeeper are allowed in the penalty area until the ball has been kicked. A penalty is an excellent chance for a team to score. Penalty-takers aim to place the ball in the corner of the net or to beat the goalkeeper with a powerful shot. Goalkeepers try to guess the direction of the ball in advance in order to make a save.

Shoot outs

A penalty shoot out is used to decide the result of a game that has ended in a tie. Teams take alternate penalties to determine the winner. If after each side has taken five penalties, the scores are even, penalties go into dramatic "sudden death." Shoot outs have been used to decide many quarter finals and semifinals and even the finals of two World Cups—the men's 1994 World Cup and the women's 1999 World Cup.

The Biggest Competition of All

The FIFA World Cup is the biggest and most prestigious soccer competition in the world. First staged in 1930 in Uruguay, it is held every four years between the world's best national teams. Brazil has won the competition five times, more than any other side. The women's World Cup began in 1991 and has become a highly popular competition with teams such as the United States, Sweden, China, and Brazil at the forefront.

Brazilian number 10, Marta, brings the ball down with her foot during a 2003 women's World Cup game against South Korea. Marta scored a penalty and her team-mate Katia struck two goals as Brazil won 3–0.

A Speedy Shot

When a penalty kick is taken, the ball can travel as fast as a car and take just a fraction of a second to reach the goal line.

Training to Play

Playing soccer at a high level requires years of training. Even the world's top players must work hard at their skills and fitness. Young players hoping to match their heroes must be prepared to practice whenever they can.

Fit for the Job

Professional soccer players spend much of their time between matches training to build their speed, strength, and stamina—the ability to work at peak performance for long periods of time. As a junior soccer player, you should not worry about strength and gym training, but you should try to get as physically fit as possible by running, taking part in other sports, and playing lots of practice matches, as well as performing drills in training or with friends.

Getting Warmer

Before playing a match or training, always warm up and stretch beforehand. This helps loosen your muscles and get your blood pumping around your body, preparing it for the physical challenge ahead. Warming up involves exercises such as running on the spot, jogging around the field, and star jumps. These should be followed by a series of back, side, groin, and upper and lower leg-muscle stretches performed under the eye of your coach.

Stretches

These players perform a series of stretches to the key muscles in their legs, arms, and back before starting a game. These stretches help them perform at their best and help prevent injuries.

Mia Hamm

Date of birth: March 17, 1972

Nationality: American

Position: Striker

Height: 5 ft 5 in (1.65 m)

International caps: 276

Goals: 158

Through training hard and practicing, Mia Hamm became the youngest-ever American women's team player when she made her debut at the age of 15. She proved a lethal goalscorer and holds the world record for international goals. Part of a gifted U.S. women's team, which won both the 1991 and 1999 World Cup, Hamm also won two Olympic gold medals for soccer.

Kit and Color

In matches, your team must all wear the same color strip (uniform), consisting of shirts, shorts, and socks. Socks are kept up with elastic or tape. Inside the socks, good shin pads, which protect the bony front of your lower leg, should be worn. In training and practice matches, wear comfortable clothing that is not too tight. A tracksuit is very useful to keep you warm before and after games or training. Do not forget a water bottle, and take regular sips in training.

These soccer players are playing a "pass and move" exercise in a small area marked with cones. They are practicing making short, accurate passes, then moving quickly into the space in time to receive a return pass.

A Good Fit

Good soccer shoes are essential. Do not be concerned whether they are endorsed by a star player. What matters is that they your foot well. A good shoe should be flexible, support your ankle well, and be made from soft leather that lets your foot feel the ball— important for passes, shots, and cushioning the ball. Shoes come with plastic studs molded into the sole or with screw-in studs. Ask your coach if your studs are the right length for the field and make sure they are all screwed in firmly.

Ball Control

You can be the greatest at passing or shooting in the world, but unless you can control the ball well, you will not have much chance to show your skills. Work on your ball-control skills before and during training and matches.

First Touch

A ball often comes toward you at high speed. Sometimes, it can be knocked onward by giving it a light touch, or glance, off your head or foot. Many times, though, you need to bring the ball under control so that it is at your feet, allowing you to pass, cross, or shoot. A ball that is gently rolling across the field can be stopped by putting your foot on the top of the ball. This is called trapping.

Cushioning not Pushing

Cushioning is a way of slowing the ball down. You need to keep your body relaxed so that the ball does not fly or bounce off. As the ball makes contact with a part of your body, you bring that part of your body back and down to cushion the ball's impact.

Body Works

Unless you are a goalkeeper, your hands and arms are the only parts of your body that you cannot use to touch and control the ball. Touching the ball deliberately with your hands or arms will result in the referee blowing the whistle for handball and giving a free kick or penalty to the other side. When the ball falls from a high position, you can use your chest or your thigh to bring the ball down under control.

Sidefoot Cushion

1 *The inside part of your shoe can be used to cushion the ball. Here, the player has turned his foot outward, presenting the inside of his show to the ball.*

2 *Keeping his balance, the player brings his foot back and down as the ball makes impact.*

3 *The ball drops to the ground allowing him to move it away with the outside of his foot.*

AC Milan midfielder Kaka performs a chest cushion. He leans back as the ball arrives to kill its speed. The ball will drop to the ground in front of him for his feet to control.

What Next?

Once the ball is under control at your feet, you have several options. Look up and be aware of what is happening on the field. If a teammate is free and in a promising position, you can make a quick, accurate pass. If there is plenty of space ahead, you can run with the ball or, if you are close to goal, you can strike a shot. If an opponent is closing in on you, look to make a clearance upfield. If you are under a lot of pressure and in danger of losing the ball, put the ball out of play for a throw-in or corner to the other team.

Thigh Cushion

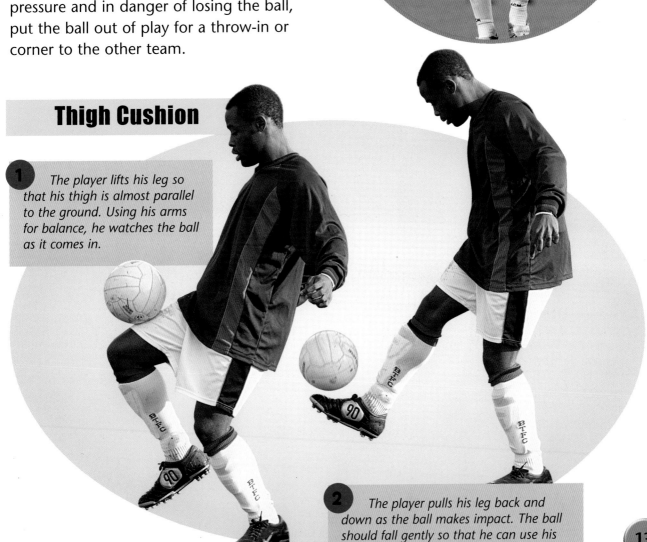

1 *The player lifts his leg so that his thigh is almost parallel to the ground. Using his arms for balance, he watches the ball as it comes in.*

2 *The player pulls his leg back and down as the ball makes impact. The ball should fall gently so that he can use his feet to get it under control.*

13

Passing

When one team has the ball under control, it is said to be in the team's possession. Once in possession, the players can move the ball around the field by passing it to each other. Good, accurate passing allows a team to stay in possession as it builds an attack.

Pass Types

The most common pass is the side-foot pass. It works well for distances up to about 65 ft (20 m) or so. It can also be used for close, accurate shots on goal. The instep drive (see page 15) is used for longer passes and shots.

Zinedine Zidane

Date of birth: June 23, 1972

Nationality: French

Position: Midfielder

Height: 6 ft (1.85 m)

International caps: 99

Goals: 27

One of the most skillful players of the past 20 years, Zidane has incredible awareness and superb passing and ball skills. He is able to unlock the tightest of defenses with a swerving run or a delicate pass. A World Cup winner with France in 1998, three years later he became the world's most expensive player when he moved to Real Madrid for more than $94 million.

Side-foot Pass

1 The player places his spare (right) foot beside the ball. He turns his passing foot outward so the inside of his shoe will make contact with the ball. The passing foot is parallel to the ground.

2 With his body over the ball, the player swings his foot, stroking through the middle of the ball. The passing foot follows through and points to the pass's target.

Instep Drive

1 The player plants his standing foot beside the ball and swings his kicking leg back.

2 The player smoothly swings his foot through the middle of the ball. He aims to make contact with the middle and lower half of his boot laces.

The player uses his arms for balance.

3 The kicking foot and leg follow through smoothly.

The Right Strength

Players can vary the speed and distance of a pass by swinging their leg back more or less and bringing their kicking foot down faster or slower through the ball. Judging how much force is needed to make a pass is vital. It comes only with a lot of practice.

Adding Height

Sometimes it is necessary to hit the ball a bit higher in the air, particularly for defensive clearances and crosses when the ball is put into the penalty area for an attacker to head or shoot. With the instep drive, the player can get extra height on the ball by leaning back a little and hitting through the lower half of the ball.

Practice Makes Perfect

It is important to practice your passing as often as possible. Passing in triangles with two teammates, as the three of you jog and sprint around the field, is a good way to practice passing to team mates while they are on the move.

Feet First

Coaches are extremely keen on players working on their passing with their weaker foot. This is because a player who can play and pass equally well with both their right and left foot is a real asset to any team.

15

On the Ball

When players receive the ball, they have to be aware of what is happening on the field. They have to watch for approaching opponents and spot where their teammates are. Keeping control of the ball, and turning and running with it are all essential skills.

Shielding

Shielding the ball is a way of preventing an opponent from getting to the ball. A player puts his body between the ball and the opponent, making it easier to keep possession.

Turning

When they have the room around them, a player can turn with the ball simply by rolling it to one side with the sole of their boot and swiveling their body to move in another direction. When space is tight, they can use a skill called a hook turn. The player leans in the direction they wish to turn. They hook their boot around the ball and as their body turns, they drag or flick the ball in the same direction with their foot.

Shielding

1 To shield the ball, the player positions his body between the ball and the player from the other team. The shielding player must not back into or push his opponent but he can keep his arms out for balance.

2 The player keeps aware of where his opponent is and keeps moving to keep his body between the opponent and the ball. He must keep the ball under control and make his next move, such as a pass back. If his opponent comes around the side, he may be able to turn the other way and sprint clear.

Running with the Ball

When players receive the ball, they will often look to run with the ball into the space ahead of them. They keep their head up as much as possible to watch how the game is developing in front of them. The key skill is to maintain their speed by pushing the ball far enough ahead of them to allow them to run well, but not so far that they lose control of the ball.

Dribbling

Dribbling is running with the ball but with the player keeping it under close control with a series of small taps and nudges.

Dribbling can be fun and looks exciting, but it is a risky move as an opponent may win the ball with a tackle. Dribbling is best done when attacking and in the other side's half of the field.

Dummying

Good dribbling often requires a lot of speed or trickery. Players may twist and turn while dribbling and may also use dummies to trick opponents. A simple dummy is to drop one shoulder and lean in one direction. This may make the opponent think you are heading one way, only for you to twist and move away in another direction.

Dummying

1 *The player on the ball drops his right shoulder and appears to be heading to his left. The defender starts to lean that way to cover his opponent's run.*

2 *The attacker pushes off his left foot sharply to head to his right. The defender has been wrong-footed and is off balance. The attacker can run past.*

Attacking

A moment of individual brilliance or skill in attack can sometimes create a good chance to score a goal. However, most goals come as a result of players working hard as a team to build attacks.

Space and Pace

As an attack develops, attackers look for areas of space into which they can run to receive the ball.

Frequently, an attacker is marked closely by a defender. They try to get free of their marker by pretending to move in one direction, only to cut away and sprint hard in a different direction.

Working Together

Attackers can work together to create a good goalscoring chance. One method is called an overlap. This is where an attacker runs down the side of the field to receive the ball. This player may then be able to continue and cross the ball into the penalty area.

Pelé

Date of birth: October 23rd, 1940

Nationality: Brazilian

Position: Striker

Height: 5 ft 9 in (1.78 m)

International caps: 92

Goals: 77

To most people, Pelé is the greatest soccer player who ever lived. A strong, amazingly skillful attacker, he possessed great awareness of others on the field. He also was blessed with a flair for doing the unexpected. He used these abilities to score more than 1,000 goals for one Brazilian club, Santos, as well as becoming the Brazilian national team's all-time leading scorer. Pelé remains the youngest goalscorer at the World Cup Finals (age 17) and won three World Cups with Brazil (in 1958, 1962, and 1970). When he retired from Santos in 1974, the club also retired his famous number 10 shirt.

Cutting Away from a Marker

The attacker (in blue) spots his teammate on the ball and looks to get away from his marker.

He starts to cut away sharply from his marker at the same time as his teammate hits a pass. He keeps his eye on the ball hoping to collect the pass.

Another method of attack is to make a run, which players from the other side follow. This can draw defenders away from an area of the field, leaving space for another attacker to run into.

One–Two Pass

The one–two or wall pass is a key way of getting past a defender and furthering an attack. A player passes to a teammate and as soon as they make the pass, they sprint past the defender.

The receiver may control the ball rapidly or may hit the ball first time. The aim is to pass the ball behind the defender and into space for the first attacker to run onto and control. One–two passes are frequently made using side-foot passes.

One-Two Pass

1 The first attacker passes to his team-mate and sprints hard past the defender.

2 The second attacker receives the ball and makes a quick, accurate pass behind the defender.

3 The first attacker runs on to the ball. He is clear of the defender who has been cut out by the two passes.

Fitness and Stamina

Experts using video cameras and computers estimate that a top male midfielder runs about seven miles (11 km) in every soccer game.

Goalscoring

Goalscoring requires an eye for a goal chance and the skill to take that chance with a shot or header. Goals can be spectacular long-range shots or simple tap-ins. Being in the right position at the right time is crucial.

A Cool Head

Players who score regularly manage to keep their cool when a chance arrives. They have to weigh up the situation very quickly and decide where to aim and what sort of shot to use. In many attacks, a chance to hit a shot disappears as quickly as it occurs. A player has to decide to shoot rapidly or pass to a teammate in a better position than themselves.

Hot Shots

A shot needs the right mixture of power and accuracy. Sometimes, a shot can be steered into a corner from close range with a side-foot pass. At other times, a more powerful shot is required. Top strikers try to aim for the part of the goal the goalkeeper is farthest away from or least expects the ball to go. If unsure, you should aim for the corners of the goal.

British player Wayne Rooney keeps his eye on the ball as he completes a shot on goal. Notice how his foot points in the direction of the shot.

On Target

Junior players sometimes find that many of their shots sail high or wide of the target. Practice is the key to good shooting as well as remembering a number of key points:

- Hit through the middle of the ball not the side or the bottom of it.
- Plant your standing foot beside the ball with your toes pointing to the target.
- Avoid leaning back or stretching for the shot.
- Keep your eyes on the ball throughout the shot.

Heading for Goal

Heading is used in many situations in a game, from clearing the ball out of defense (see page 23) to making a pass to a team-mate. When aiming to score a goal with a header, players try hard to get over the ball and keep their header down.

Goals from Free kicks

Free kicks from around the penalty area offer a good chance for a shot at goal, but the defensive team will often try to block the shot by arranging players into a defensive wall. One way of beating the wall is to pass the ball to the side so another attacker can have a clear shot at goal. Another way is to bend the ball around the wall using an outside or inside swerve shot. Swerves are very tricky skills to learn. To bend the ball with the outside of your right foot, for example, kick through the left side of the ball with the outside of the boot. Your kicking foot should follow through across your body and the ball should fly away, heading first to the left before bending to the right during its flight.

Heading Down

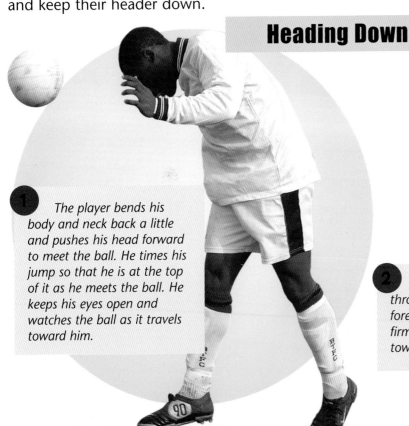

1 The player bends his body and neck back a little and pushes his head forward to meet the ball. He times his jump so that he is at the top of it as he meets the ball. He keeps his eyes open and watches the ball as it travels toward him.

2 Slightly above the ball, he pushes through the ball with the middle of his forehead. He tries to keep his neck muscles firm to direct the ball forward and down toward the goal.

Defending

When teammates lose possession of the ball, they have to start defending. Players must work as a team to stop their opponents from scoring and to try to win the ball back.

Defenders

Most teams play with four defenders (see page 6), two center backs in the middle of the defense and two fullbacks, one for each side of the field. The center backs have to be very good at heading the ball so they can deal with crosses into the penalty area. Fullbacks have to patrol their side of the field and be good at jockeying (see below) and tackling as well as being able to pass or carry the ball forward to start an attack.

Teamwork and Marking

Defending is not just for the defenders. The whole side must work together to defend. Teammates get themselves between the attack and their goal and may man-mark opponents. This means staying relatively close to an opponent to make it hard for them to receive the ball and staying between them and the goal to make it hard for them to score.

Jockeying

When you are the nearest defender to the opponent with the ball, try to close him down (get a yard or so away from him) and delay his progress. This technique is called jockeying and it can often pressure the attacker into making a mistake. Jockeying an opponent can give your teammates time to get themselves into good defensive positions and to support you.

Jockeying

The defender closest to the opponent keeps his eye on the ball as he jockeys his opponent. He stays balanced and ready to move in any direction.

A second defender moves in to support his teammate.

Defensive Header

This defender makes a defensive clearing header, using his forehead slightly tilted back to send the ball up and away from his side's penalty area.

Paolo Maldini

Date of birth: June 26, 1968

Nationality: Italian

Position: Center back or full-back

Height: 6 ft (1.85 m)

International caps: 126

Goals: 7

Capable of playing center back, but best known as a fullback, Paolo Maldini became the first defender to win *World Soccer* magazine's player of the year in 1994. An athletic defender, good in the air, and brilliant at making clean tackles, Maldini stayed at one club, AC Milan, throughout his long career, playing almost 600 games for them. He also appeared in four World Cups and four European Championships before retiring from international soccer in 2002.

Clearing the Ball

Kicks or headers can be used to clear the ball away from your own goal and out of danger. If you find yourself under pressure, consider putting the ball out for a throw-in or hitting it long up the field. When you have time on the ball, aim to pass to one of your team-mates who is in space.

Setting a Record

Scottish defender Gary Gillespie became what is believed to be the world's youngest captain in professional soccer when he captained Falkirk in 1977 at the age of 17.

Tackling

The aim of tackling is to remove the ball from another player's possession. Ideally, by tackling your opponent you will gain possession of the ball. All players, not just defenders, need to know how to make good, clean tackles that will win the ball without fouling the opponent.

Block Tackle

The most commonly used tackle is called the block tackle. It can be used from the front or from the side and, done well, will enable you to come away with the ball under your control.

Quick Thinking

Sometimes, quick thinking can be enough to win the ball without tackling. For example, an opponent may control the ball poorly or push it too far ahead of their feet. A quick-thinking defender may be able to nip in and get to the ball first.

Front Block Tackle

1 In the front block tackle, the tackler (right) moves close to the opponent and gets his body weight over the foot with which he is going to make the tackle.

2 Using the inside of his foot, and with the foot level with the field, the tackler strikes the center of the ball firmly. This removes the ball from the opponent's control.

3 Having released the ball, the tackler (in blue) seeks to get the ball under control and moves away from his opponent.

Italian defender, Fabio Cannavaro, makes a strong sliding tackle to rob Croatia's Ivica Olic of the ball. In a sliding tackle, the defender slides across the ground to hook the ball away from the opponent's feet. Sliding tackles should be used only when other, safer types of tackle cannot be performed.

Interception

Good players stay alert for the chance of a weak pass or one that is not on target. They may be able to charge in and make an interception—taking the ball away before it reaches an opponent.

Poke Tackle

A poke tackle occurs when the ball is stabbed away from an opponent, usually with the toe or instep of the boot nearest the ball. It can be useful to remove the ball from an attacker's control but does not guarantee that the ball ends up under your control. Poke tackles are often used to stop a winger heading down the sideline, by pushing the ball out for a throw-in.

Falling Foul

Tackles have to be very well timed, otherwise there is the danger of giving away a foul (see page 8). This can lead to a free kick close to your goal or, worse, a penalty. Aim to make contact with the ball first, not the player, and do not kick, shove, or pull your opponent. Whenever possible, try to make a tackle that leaves you standing on your feet, ready for the next piece of action.

Defenders on the Attack

Defenders not only prevent goals, but they can also score them. Defender, Ronald Koeman, of Holland, scored an amazing 193 goals in 533 league games between 1980 and 1997.

Goalkeeping

A goalkeeper's job is like no other soccer player's. They must organize their team's defense and use great skill, awareness, and sometimes bravery to stop goals.

Backpass Rule

A goalkeeper is the only player allowed to handle the ball—but only inside his own penalty area. The only time the goalkeeper is not allowed to handle the ball is when a teammate passes the ball back to the goalkeeper using a foot or leg. Then the keeper must kick, head, or chest the ball clear. This is known as the backpass rule.

Ball-handling

As the keeper tries to catch the ball, he always keeps his eyes on it. Whenever possible, he also tries to get his body behind the ball to act as a second barrier. His hands have their fingers spread around the back and sides of the ball, which is gathered into his body to protect it.

Keepers stay alert at all times and on the balls of their feet when facing an attack. When they have to make a diving save, they take a step toward the side of the goal to which the ball is heading and then spring off the foot nearest the ball. Catching the ball or using the palm of the hand to push it around the post, keepers try to land on their side with their body relaxed as they hit the ground.

Palm or Punch

Sometimes, a keeper cannot be sure he can catch the ball. In these cases, he has two options. He can punch the ball firmly away from the danger area. Keepers try to use both hands to clear the ball a long distance. They may also use their hands to push or palm the ball around the post or crossbar.

British player David Seaman is at full stretch as he makes a diving save from a penalty. He keeps his eyes on the ball and looks to deflect the shot around the post.

26

Ball in Play

Once the ball in is a keeper's hands, he has six seconds to release it back into play. Goalkeepers have a choice of throwing or kicking the ball to one of their teammates. A quick, accurate pass or throw can help start an attack.

For an underarm throw, the keeper bends his knees as he bowls the ball out with his arm following through to point in the direction of the target. It is the most accurate throw but can only be used over shorter distances.

Taking a High Ball

1   *A high ball such as a cross can be caught by a keeper. The keeper turns his body to face the ball and times his jump off one foot, stretching his arms up and outward.*

2   *The keeper aims to meet the ball at its highest point and tries to catch it in front of his head if possible. Once safely caught, he bends his elbows to bring the ball into his body.*

3   *As he falls, the keeper gathers the ball safely into his body.*

Statistics and Records

The FIFA World Cup

Date	Winners	Runners Up
1930	Uruguay	Argentina
1934	Italy	Czechoslovakia
1938	Italy	Hungary
1950	Uruguay	Brazil
1954	West Germany	Hungary
1958	Brazil	Sweden
1962	Brazil	Czechoslovakia
1966	England	West Germany
1970	Brazil	Italy
1974	West Germany	Netherlands
1978	Argentina	Netherlands
1982	Italy	West Germany
1986	Argentina	West Germany
1990	West Germany	Argentina
1994	Brazil	Italy
1998	France	Brazil
2002	Brazil	Germany

Most Goals in International Soccer

Women's: 158 Mia Hamm (USA)

Men's: 106 Ali Daei (Iran)

Longest Clean Sheet (no goal let in) in International Soccer:

1,142 minutes—Dino Zoff (Italy)

Most Goals in a World Cup Finals Game

12 goals (Austria 7, Switzerland 5), 1954 World Cup

Most Goals by one Player at a Single World Cup

13—Just Fontaine (France), 1958 World Cup

Most Goals in World Cup Finals in Total

14—Gerd Muller (West Germany), 1970 and 1974 World Cups

World Record Transfer Fee

$94.5 million—Zinedine Zidane, from Juventus to Real Madrid, 9th July 2001

Women's World Cup

Date	Winners	Runners Up
1991	USA	Norway
1995	Norway	Germany
1999	USA	China
2003	Germany	Sweden

Most International Caps

Women's: 282 Kristine Lilly (USA)

Men's: 173 Mohammed Al-Deayea (Saudi Arabia)

England: 125 Peter Shilton

Scotland: 102 Kenny Dalglish

Wales: 92 Neville Southall

Northern Ireland: 119 Pat Jennings

Glossary

Booking An official warning to a player given by the referee.

Clearance Kicking or heading the ball out of defense.

Cross Sending the ball from the sideline to the center of the field, usually into the other team's penalty area.

Cushioning Slowing a ball down to control it by using a part of your body.

Dribbling Moving the ball under close control with a series of taps and nudges.

Foul To break one of the rules of soccer.

Instep The top of your boot where the laces are.

Interception When a player gets to an opponent's pass first and steals the ball.

Jockeying The skill of delaying an opponent with the ball.

Marking Standing close to and guarding a member of the other team while that team attacks.

Penalty kick A free shot at goal taken from the penalty spot.

Referee's assistants Two officials who help the referee to run a match.

Shielding Placing your body (without committing a foul) between the ball and an opposition player to protect the ball.

Tackling Using your feet to take the ball away from an opponent.

Web sites

www.fifa.com/en/index.html
The official web site for the organization that runs world soccer, FIFA's website includes news, features, and details of all World Cups.

www.uefa.com
The homepage of the Union of European Football Associations, the organization that runs the European Championship and the Champions League.

www.thefa.com
Home of the English Football Association with news on the England national team, clubs, and league tables and the FA Cup.

www.shekicks.net
This web site offers in-depth coverage of women's soccer with links to club and competition web sites.

www.bettersoccermorefun.com
A web site full of great coaching tips and tactics.

www.soccerlinks.net
A huge treasure chest of links to over 900 soccer-related websites.

www.ussoccer.com
The official site of U.S. Soccer and the U.S. Men's and Women's National Teams

Note to parents and teachers: every effort has been made by the Publishers to ensure that these web sites are suitable for children, that they are of the highest educational value, and that they contain no inappropriate or offensive material. However, because of the nature of the Internet, it is impossible to guarantee that the contents of these sites will not be altered. We strongly advise that Internet access is supervised by a responsible adult.

Index